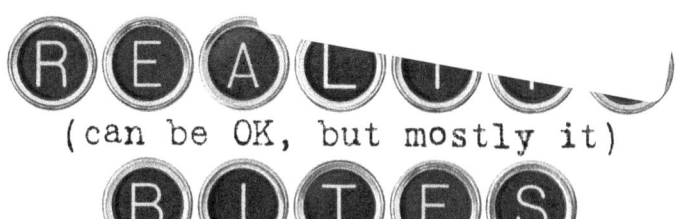

# REALITY
(can be OK, but mostly it)
# BITES

For Evan

May he plumb the joys of words
and the realities of life

Copyright © 2015, 2021 Gordon Hutchison
All rights reserved.

Published 2021 by White River Press
PO Box 3561, Amherst, MA 01004
whiteriverpress.com

ISBNs:  978-1-887043-90-8   paperback
        978-1-887043-91-5   ebook

Book layout and cover design by Lufkin Graphic Designs
Norwich, VT • www.LufkinGraphics.com


Library of Congress Cataloging-in-Publication Data

Names: Hutchison, Gordon Ross, 1949- author.
Title: Reality (can be ok, but mostly it) bites : original aphorisms and
  other philosophical fragments with teeth / Gordon Hutchison.
Description: Amherst, Massachusetts : White River Press, 2021. | Includes
  index.
Identifiers: LCCN 2021003614 (print) | LCCN 2021003615 (ebook) | ISBN
  9781887043908 (paperback) | ISBN 9781887043915 (ebook)
Subjects: LCSH: Aphorisms and apothegms.
Classification: LCC PN6271 .H88 2021  (print) | LCC PN6271  (ebook) | DDC
  082--dc23
LC record available at https://lccn.loc.gov/2021003614
LC ebook record available at https://lccn.loc.gov/2021003615

# REALITY
(can be OK, but mostly it)
# BITES

Original aphorisms and other
philosophical fragments with teeth

# GORDON HUTCHISON

White River Press
Amherst, Massachusetts

# Introduction

Not everyone can rattle off a credible definition of the word "aphorism," but chances are they'll recognize one when they see it.

### If it ain't broke, don't fix it.
*Thomas Bertram Lance*

According to the Oxford Dictionary, an aphorism is "a pithy observation that contains a general truth." My favorites are the ones I don't see coming. The ones that grab me—with unorthodox word combinations, juxtapositions, inversions of terms and other deceptive word play. The ones that make me stop, think and maybe think again: "*Wait a minute . . . what?!*"

### Time is precious, waste it wisely.
*Anonymous*

The ones I have to read slower the second time, until the "*Oh, yeah!*" light goes on. (Truth be told, sometimes it doesn't.)

### Poetry is a religion with no hope.
*Jean Cocteau*

And the ones that have me laughing out loud before I can clap a hand over my mouth.

> **Modern art is what happens when painters stop looking at girls and persuade themselves they have a better idea.**
>
> *John Anthony Ciardi*

My preference for some types implies there are others. Quite a few, in fact; in his *Geary's Guide to the World's Great Aphorists*, James Geary defines eight: the Chiasmus, the Definition, the Joke, the Metaphor, the Moral, the Observation, the Paradox and the Pensée. Some are relatively straightforward, others deliciously convoluted.

There is also a confusing glut of *non*-aphorisms; Geary lists adages, apothegms, axioms, bromides, dictums, epigrams, mottoes, parables, platitudes, precepts, proverbs, quips, quotations, sound bites, slogans, truisms and witticisms. Considering the blurred distinctions, overlapping boundaries and conflicting definitions, this family of wit is too unwieldy to examine here. Besides, given its history—dating back 5,000 years to ancient China—it's the aphorism that holds the distinction of the world's oldest literary genre, the primal ancestor, the root of the family tree. Now the question becomes, just what gives an aphorism its snap, crackle and pop?

# The Aphorism According to Geary

**1. It Must Be Brief:** Aphorisms got their start in China, but saw use throughout the ancient world—a world where books were virtually non-existent and literacy limited to a scholarly elite. As the teachings of sages and scholars in cultures relying on oral transmission, the key to longevity was easy-to-remember. And the key to easy-to-remember was short, catchy and relevant.

The great religious masters excelled at phrasing their teachings in terms simple, uneducated people could understand. With down-to-earth wit and imagery, they crafted messages that had practical value based on applicability to people's lives. Catchy? Check. Relevant? Check.

But first and foremost, oral transmissions had to be short. Unlike the more lengthy sutra, which required memorization by monks, religious "professionals," aphorisms targeted specific situations. With catchy phrasing and relevant content, their brevity ensured the ease of recall crucial to long shelf life with the audiences of the ages. That formula remains valid today, with aphorisms ranging in length from a few words to a few sentences.

> **He is a benefactor of mankind who contracts the great rules of life into short sentences, that may be easily impressed on the memory, and so recur habitually to the mind.**
> *Samuel Johnson*

**2. It Must Be Definitive:** Like definitions, aphorisms "assert rather than argue, proclaim rather than persuade, declare rather than suggest." Their authors aren't opening the floor for discussion; they're telling it like it is—at least like *they* see it. The pronouncements of ancient wise men, the original aphorists, carried great weight in their day—much like quotes from celebrities, business magnates and politicians today. I have seen aphorisms I disagreed with, but they were without doubt the author's truth.

**3. It Must Be Personal:** Geary calls aphorisms "the most intimate, idiosyncratic literary genre." They are unique to the individual, springing from personal philosophies built over years of experience. Which is why aphorisms are, for the most part, ascribable to specific authors. While compiling this book, I realized that many sayings coined from my own ideology of life qualified as standalone aphorisms. Taken as a whole, they commemorate many milestones—changes, realizations, victories and setbacks—on my road to today.

**4. It Must Have A Twist:** There are twists and there are twists, but they all share one element: the unexpected. A good aphorism features a verbal or psychological flip, a sting, a shock, a jolt. It could be a reversal of expectations—setting up the reader to go in one direction, then hijacking him in another.

> **As long as the heart preserves desire,
> the mind preserves illusion.**
>
> *François-René de Chateaubriand*

The twist could also involve juxtaposing two things people don't commonly associate or revealing unnoticed correspondences.

> **A translation, like a wife, is seldom strictly faithful
> if it is in the least attractive.**
>
> *Anonymous*

Or the cunning use of paradox or inversion of terms.

> **War does not determine who is right—
> only who is left.**
>
> *Bertrand Russell*

Some twists are more twisted than others, of course. And yes, there have been quite a few I haven't gotten at all, no matter how many times I reread them.

**5. It Must Be Philosophical:** According to J.S. Mill, aphorisms are "the literary form in which the wisdom of the ages most embodies itself." Maybe in the beginning, but not today—at least not across the board. While aphorisms might have started out as bearers of eternal, immutable truths, centuries of secularization have seen the transition to, in some cases, little more than strong opinions. So what is "philosophical?" Wisdom limited to eternal, immutable truths? Or does it include more personal, "relative" truths, the kind forced to win acceptance on the competitive marketplace of ideas? For me, this is Geary's most problematic category, in that the criterion to qualify one saying and disqualify another is not entirely clear. But then, so what?

## Aphorisms, God, and the Devil

Aphorisms date back to the oral cultures of antiquity, yet feature remarkable consistency of thematic content—for the most part, biting exposés of the contradictions, hypocrisy, inequality, folly and other signature foibles of the human tragicomedy. In debunking these shortcomings, aphorisms are part of the Western approach to problem solving—identifying issues, getting them out in the open as the first step toward finding solutions, "undoing" mistakes, righting wrongs.

> **A problem adequately stated is a problem well on its way to being solved.**
> *R. Buckminster Fuller*

In Christianity, with its signature dichotomy of good and evil, concealment signifies the Devil's work. Lies began as man's attempt to cover up his violations of God's commandments—the commission of evil. Cosmic order is predicated on keeping these commandments, chaos the consequence of breaking them. And since violations are the result of man's inability to resist the Devil's temptations, any form of discord—corruption, injustice, exploitation—falls squarely in Lucifer's domain. Man does God's work when he exposes the Devil's by bringing it out of the unholy darkness and into the holy light. In modern terms, identification, clarification and assessment are the requisite first steps in conquering evil and its hold on God's children. This approach is the foundation of Western traditions from confession in the Catholic Church to Freud's approach to defusing neuroses and corporate culture's playbook of conflict resolution.

## Aphorism as entertainment, aphorism as comfort, aphorism as resistance

In the best aphorisms, the twist grabs the reader's attention, the attention focuses the mind on the message, and the message sinks in. If the truth hits home, for that fleeting instant the reader becomes incrementally more aware. (Not that all "truths" are true, of course.) The unfortunate reality, however, is that, in pointing out problems, aphorisms, despite their distinguished authors and long history, do little more than point. As history shows, problems don't go away no matter how many aphorisms you throw at them. Humanity's hide is too thick; the people who should be listening aren't. Considering that the world's most fertile minds have produced aphorisms with similar content for millennia, their efficacy as instruments of social change is clearly nill.

So what good *are* aphorisms? Well, they make us *feel* good, or at least better. They delight us with their wit and word play—their entertainment value. On a deeper level, they unite us in the knowledge that we're not the only ones unhappy at the mess the human race has made of things. Small consolation, but they let us know we're in good company. Sensible, rational men have always constituted a frustrated minority, and there is some illusory solace in the thought that many of the great minds of history felt as helpless as we do.

> **There are times when one would like to hang the whole human race, and finish the farce.**
>
> *Mark Twain*

> **Every normal man must be tempted, at times, to spit on his hands, hoist the black flag, and begin slitting throats.**
>
> *H. L. Mencken*

This brings us to aphorism as palliative. Beneath the entertainment value lies the defense mechanism—laughing to keep from crying, a band-aid on the inevitable despair of following the road signs of civilization to their logical destination. Aphorisms' power to make us feel better comes from our desire to believe, despite all indications to the contrary, that "everything will be all right"—that truth and good guys will triumph in the end. They give us the false sense of security that fleeting awareness of problems can and will accomplish something. At that deeper level, aphorisms are token resistance to a world gone mad, a symbolic stand against the relentless onslaught of man against himself.

## This book

Between the 1600s and 1800s, what Geary calls the "golden age of aphorism in Europe," a well-received collection of aphorisms could make a literary career. Not so much today; like jazz, the genre's ship has sailed. Compilations, collections and anthologies today target niche interest groups and public speakers in working their audiences. Appreciation of this art form for its own sake brands one as "curious," while those who proactively employ them to decry human frailties are labeled "curmudgeons" or "misanthropes."

So, what will you find in this book? That largely depends on you. To appreciate its 400 entries, you'll need a robust sense of irony, a love of word play and a healthy helping of resignation. Some qualify as aphorisms, several with a downright "classical" ring, while others don't even start to satisfy Geary's criteria. You'll find irreverent pronouncements, devil's advocate laments that mean the opposite of what they say and queries that rely on readers' having shared the same experience or feelings. I began jotting them down as they came to me back in the mid-1990s, decades before discovering a Pensée or Chiasmus and years before I could coherently discuss an aphorism at all.

Some aphorists, or whatever you call them these days, impose rules on their work. Ashley Brilliant, for instance, limits his messages to seventeen words, presumably from the seventeen-syllable format of Japanese haiku poems. Mine have no rules. When reading other people's efforts, however, I do find my attention fading after the second line, so I try to keep them short. I also try to keep the tone relatively light, avoiding darker themes if I can't sugar coat them with humor or, at least, irony.

## Where have I heard that before?

I have mentioned the striking thematic consistency of aphorisms down through the ages—not only content, but techniques of expression, no matter what era they're from. One reason for this uniformity is that the human animal hasn't changed, which has made it easier for great minds to think alike.

But how often does it go beyond mere thinking to outright taking? As the easiest literary genre to remember, aphorisms are also the easiest to rip off. Nor were the great aphorists strangers to this temptation. Although Ralph Waldo Emerson's lament might not qualify as an aphorism, it might be the most to-the-point:

**All my best thoughts were stolen by the ancients.**

Benjamin Franklin, for one, confessed to frequent borrowing, adapting and condensing of old English proverbs and other sayings.

There have been others.

> **Originality is the art of concealing your sources.**
> *Attributed to many sources*

> **About the most originality any writer can hope to achieve honestly is to steal with good judgment.**
> *Josh Billings*

In *The Harper Book of Quotations*, editor Robert Fitzhenry presents graphic examples of this "sharing" down through the ages. "Pygmies placed on the shoulders of giants see more than the giants themselves," for instance, originally ascribed to Roman poet Marcus Lucan (39-65), was resurrected almost word for word fifteen centuries later by Robert Burton (1577-1640): "A dwarf standing on the shoulders of giants sees farther than a giant himself." From there, it was appropriated by the redoubtable Sir Isaac Newton (1642-1727): "If I have seen farther, it is by standing on the shoulders of giants." Fortunately for the Renaissance literati, the Internet hadn't been invented yet.

And how many proud Americans would be shocked to learn that Abraham Lincoln's most unforgettable line was not his own? That's right, "government of the people, by the people, for the people," did not originate with Honest Abe, but with the Bible—the general prologue of the 1384 Wycliffe translation, at least: "This

Bible is for the government of the people, by the people and for the people." The fact that the great thinkers of the past were more intimately acquainted with the Bible than those of today makes it hard not to wonder if they didn't interpret the passage, "And there is no new thing under the sun," (Ecclesiastes 1:9) too literally.

Geary presents an interesting treatment of aphorism-cloning in his *Guide to the World's Great Aphorists*. After presenting the representative work of each author, he includes similar sayings from others in sections he calls, "Parallel Lines." Having come across a startling number of classic aphorisms startlingly close to mine, I have followed Geary's example and included those I've found. I can say with clear conscience that I have never plagiarized another's work. Nonetheless, if you find that claim difficult to believe as you read, I've collected the evidence for you.

**"The mind can hold so much that means so little."**
*Gordon Hutchison*

**"Lots of knowledge fits into a hollow head."**
*Karl Kraus*

## That's all, folks

I'd like to close with two thoughts. The first, from arguably America's preeminent aphorist, foreshadows Freud while echoing the sages and mystics of history. The implication, that man lacks control of his desires, actions and destiny, is cloaked in a bon mot as concise as it is problematic to dispute:

> **When we remember we are all mad, the mysteries of life disappear and life stands explained.**
>
> *Mark Twain*

The second, which might or might not be an aphorism in its own right, turns the reader's presumed fondness for aphorisms back on himself, though more as compliment than criticism:

> **To appreciate twists, you must be twisted.**
>
> *Gordon Hutchison*

# Reality (...) Bites

1  Life is a series of progressively less successful ventures in crisis management.

※

2  The first rule of anything should be to throw away the rules.

※

3  To know a man, find his motives. To control him, find his pleasures.

> In the works of mankind, it is the motive which is chiefly worth attention.
> *Johann Wolfgang von Goethe, 1749-1834*
>
> **No man is a hypocrite in his pleasures.**
> *Samuel Johnson, 1709-1784*

4 If you can't say something nice, say it first.

☙

5 Home is the closest thing to a womb you can still get back into.

> Home is the place, when you have to go there, they have to take you in.
> *Robert Frost, 1874-1963*
>
> Humans are the only creatures on Earth that allow children to come back home.
> *Bill Cosby, 1937—*

☙

6 Two wrongs might not make a right, but they *can* make consecutive sentences.

7   Those who feed peoples' appetites never go hungry.

> Whatever will satisfy hunger is good food.
> *Chinese proverb*
>
> There are only two ways of getting on in the world: by one's own industry, or by the weaknesses of others.
> *Jean de la Bruyère, 1645-1696*

❧

8   Politicians show exemplary ingenuity and perseverance in their ongoing efforts to fool all of the people all of the time.

❧

9   Considering the popular appeal of the Ten Commandments, no wonder God hasn't put out a sequel.

> The Ten Commandments make Prohibition look like a stroke of genius.
> *Thomas Dunker*
>
> 10 was obviously too hard, so here's just 1 Commandment: Don't be an asshole.
> *Anonymous*

10 What are women if not living proof that figures speak louder than words?

> Her figure is harder to ignore than a ringing telephone.
> *Anonymous*

☙

11 Children are God's way of letting parents know if they're having a nice day.

☙

12 Most communication gaps are bridged more effectively with money than communication.

> Money is far more persuasive than logical argument.
> *Euripides, 480-406 BC*

13 Reality is rarely faced well on an empty stomach.

☙

14 Knowledge accumulates. Idiocy compounds daily.

☙

15 If you can still say no, you haven't had enough.

16 The wise learn from failure. The wisest learn from success.

> Nothing fails like success because we don't learn from it. We learn only from failure.
> *Kenneth Ewart Boulding, 1910-1993*

☙

17 Moderation is the battle cry of those who can't imagine greater.

☙

18 Old age laments the consequences of youthful excesses while regretting their departure.

19  If ignorance really *were* bliss, the world would be a much happier place.

☙

20  The more trivial or idiotic the message, the more time, effort and money people are willing to put into communicating it.

> The more trifling the subject, the more
> animated and protracted the discussion.
> *Franklin Pierce, 1804-1869*

☙

21  Kindness is what you can do the most good with the littlest of.

22  The best thing about forbidden fruit is that it never goes bad.

※

23  The line between right and wrong is all too often drawn by the hand of convenience.

> What is right is often forgotten by what is convenient.
> *Bodie Thoene 1951 —*

※

24  Some fools are smart enough to hide their foolishness, but never learned men their learning.

> He not only overflowed with learning, he stood in the slop.
> *Sydney Smith, 1771-1845*

25   Who doesn't believe that, somewhere along the line, he should've have gotten a better deal?

> **Every man thinks he deserves better.**
> *Thomas Fuller, 1608-1661*

※

26   If life is a test, make mine true or false.

※

27   Sometimes it takes more courage to do the *wrong* thing.

28 Democracy and religion simply perpetuate the myth that ordinary people matter.

> The real beauty of democracy is that the
> average man believes he is above average.
> *Morrie Brickman, 1917-1994*

※

29 Where would Christianity be without capital punishment?

※

30 Relationships would be so much more sustainable if they came with his and hers remotes.

> Sometimes I wish life had a fast-forward button.
> *Dan Chopin*

31  People who can afford to have scruples usually don't.

❧

32  To claim a monopoly on truth is to advertise pride in the inability to think.

> To be uncertain is to be uncomfortable,
> but to be certain is to be ridiculous.
> *Chinese proverb*

❧

33  Doesn't it feel great, now and then, to tell the world to go screw itself?

> Every human being must have a point at which he stands against the culture,
> where he says, this is me and the damned world can go to hell.
> *Rollo May, 1909-1994*

34 No one works harder than a lazy man at inventing new ways to avoid work.

> Work is less boring than amusing oneself.
> *Charles Baudelaire, 1821-1867*
>
> The lazy are always wanting to do something.
> *Harry Vaughan, 1893-1981*

※

35 The old assure the young they can do anything they set their minds to—unless, of course, it's something the old have their minds set against.

※

36 Medicine is still an inexact science, except when it comes to adding up the bills.

37 How many social networks will it take to prove the world has too much free time?

❦

38 If you've made friends with yourself, you're always in good company.

> A man has to live with himself; he should see that he always has good company.
> *Anonymous*

❦

39 Life is like wine tasting. You can't have it all, so taste wisely.

40  Children see what they want to, adults what they need to.

₰

41  Socialization starts before we know better and continues until we don't know shit.

₰

42  The evolution of the human intellect is the more remarkable considering the lack of corresponding gains in character.

> The human race has improved everything except the human race.
> *Adlai Stevenson, 1900-1965*
>
> The progress of science is far ahead of man's ethical behavior.
> *Charles Chaplin, 1889-1977*

43 Ever get the feeling that, somewhere along the line, there must have been a really important memo everybody got but you?

> There is a strong disposition . . . to suppose that everyone else
> is having a more enjoyable time than we are ourselves.
> *Anthony Powell, 1905-2000*

☙

44 Self-esteem begins with realizing the world is just as clueless as you are.

☙

45 Life is the kind of joke you have to be there to appreciate.

> The meaning of life cannot be told; it has to happen to a person.
> *Ira Progoff, 1921-1998*

46 $\mathbf{M}$an is the animal that *can* learn but never *does*.

※

47 $\mathrm{T}$reasure friendship, revere love, honor family, but remember: in the end, you're all you've got.

> Of my friends I am the only one I have left.
> *Terence, 190-158 BC*
>
> You are all you will ever have for certain.
> *June Havoc, 1912-2010*

※

48 $\mathrm{L}$ove demands fortitude, resilience and commitment, not brains.

> Love is like an hourglass, with the heart filling up as the brain empties.
> *Jules Renard, 1864-1910*

49 Little good—or fair—comes from well-funded minds running free.

※

50 Innocence is the art of not making the past present.

※

51 Ignorance is not so much the lack of knowledge as the audacity to act on it.

> Nothing is more terrible than ignorance in action.
> *Johann Wolfgang von Goethe, 1749-1834*
> All you need in this life is ignorance and confidence, then success is sure.
> *Mark Twain, 1835-1910*

52 Are there criteria for distinguishing a *genuine* mid-life crisis from that perennial feeling of being old, useless and unwanted?

❧

53 What is the Devil if not solid historical evidence that good help is hard to find?

❧

54 Imagine if you *hadn't* said the things you shouldn't have and *had* said the things you should . . .

> We have left undone those things which we ought to have done; and we have done those things which we ought not to have done.
> *Book of Common Prayer*

55 Realize your potential. Don't be all you never could be.

※

56 You have to *find* "well enough" before you can leave it alone.
> You never know what is enough unless you know what is more than enough.
> *William Blake, 1757-1827*
> Many of the insights of a saint stem from his experience as a sinner.
> *Eric Hoffer, 1902-1983*

※

57 Many minds are easier lost than changed.

58 Doing nothing, done right, can take all day.

> If you can spend a perfectly useless afternoon in a perfectly useless manner, you have learned how to live.
> *Lin Yutang, 1895-1976*
>
> How beautiful it is to do nothing, and then rest afterward.
> *Spanish saying*

※

59 The determination to go on living is often far more self-destructive than the alternative.

※

60 It is easier to believe a thousand agreeable lies than a single disagreeable truth.

> Flattery makes friends, and truth makes enemies.
> *Spanish proverb*
>
> Most people today don't want honest answers insofar as honest means unpleasant or disturbing.
> *Louis Kronenberger, 1904-1980*

61 Love that turns to hate is neither.
> The worst, the least curable hatred is that which has superseded deep love.
> *Euripides, 480-406 BC*
>
> Hatreds are the cinders of affections.
> *Walter Raleigh, 1552-1618*

☙

62 Is there such a thing as a born-again reincarnationist?

☙

63 Who but mothers ever imagined so much comfort in denial?

64 The thing about capitalism is, the capitalists end up with the capital.

> The forces in a capitalist society . . . tend to
> make the rich richer and the poor poorer.
> *Jawaharlal Nehru, 1889-1964*
>
> It is usually people in the money business, finance,
> and international trade that are really rich.
> *Robin Leach, 1941—*

❧

65 Did God make politicians after He discovered grading on a curve?

❧

66 Few emotions surpass anger's ability to focus the mind, but *none* outdoes its *inability* to make good decisions.

> Anger is a bad counselor.
> *French proverb*
>
> Speak when you're angry and you'll make
> the best speech you'll ever regret.
> *Groucho Marx, 1890-1977*

67 What good are people you can't blame your problems on?

> There is nothing will kill a man so soon as having nobody to find fault with but himself.
> *George Eliot, 1819-1880*

☙

68 What if evolution is nature's version of the Peter Principle?

☙

69 You only live once. If that's not enough, you're not doing it right.

70 Every unreasonable man has his reasons.

> The heart has reasons that reason knows nothing of.
> *Blaise Pascal, 1622-1662*
>
> Man is a reasoning, rather than a reasonable animal.
> *Robert B. Hamilton*

৯

71 If at first you don't succeed, call it art.

৯

72 As work expands to fill the time available, so circumstances extenuate to accommodate the vested interests involved.

73 Living things are not born equal. Or, with rights. Life isn't fair. Get over it.

> Men are made by nature unequal. It is vain,
> therefore, to treat them as if they were equal.
> *James Anthony Froude, 1818-1894*
>
> All animals are equal, but some animals are more equal than others.
> *George Orwell, 1903-1950*

※

74 Suffering, like talent, requires an audience to realize its full potential.

> It's easier to suffer in silence if you are sure someone is watching.
> *Anonymous*
>
> Misery loves company.
> *English proverb*

※

75 If nations were as committed to solving the world's problems as they are to sports, we'd have peace in no time.

> Some people think football is a matter of life and death . . .
> I can assure them it is much more serious than that.
> *Bill Shankly, 1914-1981*

76 When Christians look at the world today, do they ever wonder what God was thinking?

※

77 Solitude is the opportunity to get better acquainted with yourself. Loneliness is the failure to take advantage of that opportunity.

> Many . . . had rather meet their bitterest enemy in the field, than their own hearts in their closet.
> *Charles Caleb Colton, 1780-1832*

※

78 How much longer before politicians retire the Golden Rule as no longer politically correct, economically viable, ethically feasible or socially relevant?

79 Whoever said, "Kissing don't last. Cooking do," couldn't have gotten far past kissing.

※

80 For sages and children, all is wonder.
>To the illumined mind the whole world sparkles with light.
>*Ralph Waldo Emerson, 1803-1882*

※

81 Beware the boredom of the rich and famous.
>Ennui has made more gamblers than avarice, more drunkards than thirst, and perhaps as many suicides as despair.
>*Charles Caleb Colton, 1780-1832*

82  All the great wisdom has been said before, but much of it bears repeating.

> All intelligent thoughts have already been thought;
> what is necessary is only to try to think them again.
> *Johann Wolfgang von Goethe, 1749-1834*

☙

83  One down side of overcoming inferiority complexes is no more excuses for inferiority.

☙

84  If historians prove anything, it's that the past isn't what it used to be.

> There are lots of people who mistake their imagination for their memory.
> *Josh Billings, 1818-1885*
> The older a man gets, the farther he had to walk to school as a boy.
> *Anonymous*

85 Never put off till tomorrow what you can get out of doing altogether.

☙

86 Ever notice how the dictates of interim ethics depend entirely on the length of the interim?

☙

87 The surest way to prove what you're not is trying to prove you are.

> Nothing prevents us from being natural so much as the desire to appear so.
> *François Duc de La Rochefoucauld, 1613-1680*
> The louder he talked of his honor, the faster we counted our spoons.
> *Ralph Waldo Emerson, 1803-1882*

88 Where there's a will, there's a lawyer looking for a way.

※

89 Wouldn't it be nice if the people with all the answers waited for the questions?

※

90 Why are there so many worthy causes and so few worthy effects?

91 What are TV and social media if not the pinnacle of man's genius for making something out of nothing?

> Television has lifted the manufacture of banality out of the sphere of handicraft and placed it in that of a major industry.
> *Nathalie Sarraute, 1900-1999*

❧

92 Those who clamor for the right to free speech invoke it with the intent to exploit, provoke, slander or incite prurience. The price of rights is abuse by the unworthy.

❧

93 It's always hardest to say no to yourself.

94 Life is over before you knew it, and you weren't even having fun.

> As our life is very short, so it is very miserable, and therefore it is well it is short.
> *Jeremy Taylor, 1613-1667*
>
> Life is full of misery, loneliness and suffering—and it's all over much too soon.
> *Woody Allen, 1935—*

※

95 The difference between advice and fish is, it takes time for fish to stink.

※

96 When life stops being an exercise in discovery, it becomes an exercise in futility.

97 Little makes a man more mysterious to a woman than acting his age.

> As long as you know that most men are like children, you know everything.
> *Coco Chanel, 1883-1971*
> The American male doesn't mature until he has exhausted all other possibilities.
> *Wilfrid Sheed, 1930-2011*

☙

98 Could rap have been commissioned by parents of baby boomers as payback for rock *'n'* roll?

☙

99 Those who see the world as their oyster don't share pearls.

100 Reverence for simplicity begets wisdom.
Reverence for complexity begets science.

> Progress is man's ability to complicate simplicity.
> *Thor Heyerdahl, 1914-2002*
>
> Complexity is what interests scientists in the end, not simplicity.
> *Edward O. Wilson, 1929—*

☙

101 When are they going to start handing out Nobel Prizes for apathy and indecision?

☙

102 The man who can laugh at the world first learned to laugh at himself.

> You grow up the day you have your first real laugh—at yourself.
> *Ethyl Barrymore, 1879-1959*
>
> Happy is the person who can laugh at himself.
> *Habib Bourguiba, 1903-2000*

103 How often does leadership boil down to good guesses and a straight face?

❧

104 One of the first signs of getting old is not wanting to.

❧

105 Is it "hypocrisy" or "stupidity" to pray to a God you create yourself?

> It is convenient that there be gods, and,
> as it is convenient, let us believe that there are.
> *Ovid, 43 BC-17 AD*
>
> If triangles invented a god, they would make him three-sided.
> *Michel Eyquem de Montaigne, 1533-1592*

106 Experience simply means fewer excuses the next time.

※

107 When your body drives you to seek pleasure, shut up and enjoy the ride!

※

108 For most of us, getting what we pay for is a safer option than getting what we deserve.
> There is no man so good, who, were he to submit all his thoughts and actions to the laws, would not deserve hanging ten times in this life.
> *Michel Eyquem de Montaigne, 1533-1592*

109 Life is a never-ending procession of evanescent emotions. Unfortunately, avarice, revenge and dominance obsession have the most staying power.

110 Nothing pacifies unruly masses like a good scandal.

111 Is it that fame makes people strange, or that strange people want to be famous?

112 Man worships what he doesn't understand and can't see, and hates what he doesn't understand and can.

> Wonder is the basis of worship.
> *Thomas Carlyle, 1795-1881*
>
> We call "mystical" a connection that we feel without understanding it.
> *Isolde Kurz, 1853-1944*

※

113 Love wants itself, wants here, wants now. Beware emotions that predicate a future.

※

114 Little is more materially rewarding and spiritually crippling than privilege.

> Mind, like bodies, will often fall into a pimpled, ill-conditioned state from mere excess of comfort.
> *Charles Dickens, 1812-1870*
>
> People of privilege will always risk their complete destruction rather than surrender any material part of their advantage.
> *Romain Gary, 1914-1990*

115 Lofty ideals have long sustained dedicated combatants in lost causes far past the point where anyone with common sense would have pulled the hell out.

≶

116 When did the medical profession change its motto from "Do no harm," to "Healthy people are bad for business"?

> No doctor takes pleasure in the health even of his friends.
> *Michel Eyquem de Montaigne, 1533-1592*

≶

117 Function is beauty, its application art.

> Beauty is the purgation of superfluities.
> *Michelangelo, 1475-1564*
>
> We ascribe beauty to that which is simple; which has no superfluous parts; which exactly answers its ends.
> *Ralph Waldo Emerson, 1803-1882*

118 Historians have made a profession of talking the past to death because it can't talk back.

※

119 Prove yourself to yourself. Everything else is just showing off.

> There is nothing noble about being superior to some other man. The true nobility is in being superior to your previous self.
> *Hindu proverb*
>
> A creative man is motivated by the desire to achieve, not by the desire to beat others.
> *Ayn Rand, 1905-1982*

※

120 Humanity is what it is because we never outgrow our most cherished childhood belief: that wishing makes it so.

> Faith is the substance of things hoped for.
> *Hebrews, XI. 1*
>
> You believe that easily which you hope for earnestly.
> *Edward Bulwer-Lytton, 1803-1873*

121 Alone we can do so little. Together, we can screw up *anything*.

⁂

122 Ignorance goes beyond just not knowing. It's *refusing* to know, as in "*ignore*-ance."

> Most ignorance is vincible ignorance.
> We don't know because we don't want to know.
> *Aldous Huxley, 1894-1963*

⁂

123 *Really* bad luck is when not only the odds are against you, but the evens, too.

124 In a democracy, reality is the majority perception.

> What is morality in any given time or place? It is what the majority then and there happen to like, and immorality is what they dislike.
> *Alfred North Whitehead, 1861-1947*
>
> Reality is whatever the people around at the time agree to.
> *Milton H. Miller, 1939-2004*

※

125 The tragedy of poverty is, there comes a point after which you no longer live in it, but it lives in you.

> If you've ever really been poor, you remain poor at heart all your life.
> *Arnold Bennett, 1867-1931*
>
> America has put a tight shoe on the Negro and now he has a callous on his soul.
> *Dick Gregory, 1932—*

※

126 Without mistakes, life would *be* one.

127  Haste makes waste—and babies.

❦

128  The only thing faster than the speed at which the world keeps changing is the speed at which politicians keep screwing it up.
> The world is undergoing a transformation to which no change that has yet occurred can be compared, either in scope or in rapidity.
> *Charles de Gaulle, 1890-1970*

❦

129  Death is the common denominator of all life. No wonder more people aren't thrilled with the dividends.

130  The only things "wealth" and "truth" have in common are the final two consonants.

☙

131  If only airlines offered regularly scheduled flights from reality . . .

☙

132  There's no stronger loyalty than that of the clueless for the meaningless.

> Nothing is so firmly believed as what we least know.
> *Michel Eyquem de Montaigne, 1533-1592*
>
> When people are least sure, they are often most dogmatic.
> *John Kenneth Galbraith, 1908-2006*

133 How fleeting the steps on the journey of life from hop, skip and jump to trip, stumble and fall.

※

134 Do honest people admit the undeniable truth that, sometimes, it's better to lie?

> The lie is a condition of life.
> *Friedrich Nietzsche, 1844-1900*

※

135 To invent a corkscrew, hire a drunk.

> The best device for clearing the driveway of snow is a youth who wants to use the car.
> *Anonymous*

136  You'll never find happiness around the corner ignoring the runaway bus barreling down Main Street.

> There is one thing that gives radiance to everything.
> It is the idea of something around the corner.
> *G. K. Chesterton, 1874-1936*

☙

137  Life 101: "Just when I had it all figured out, the drugs wore off."

☙

138  There is no cure for the common fool.

139 Politicians would tax God if they thought the IRS could collect.

※

140 To beat the world, compete with yourself.

> Real winners do not compete.
> *Samuli Paronen, 1917-1974*
> You're not in competition with anyone but yourself.
> *Anonymous*

※

141 If God is so smart, why can't He make something humans *can't* screw up?

> You can't make anything idiot proof, because idiots are so ingenious.
> *Ron Burns*

142 In light of the tenacity, ferocity and ubiquity of the war of the sexes, how fortunate God stopped at two.

> Breathes there a man with skin so tough, who says two sexes aren't enough?
> *Samuel Hoffenstein, 1890-1947*

☙

143 What writer hasn't finished a book without thinking, "*That'll* show 'em."?

☙

144 Relationships 101: "Let's start over. You change."

145 Whoever said, "Honesty is the best policy," was lying.

> Few people would not be the worse for complete sincerity.
> *F. H. Bradley, 1846-1924*
>
> Let none of us delude himself by supposing that honesty is always the best policy. It is not.
> *William Ralph Inge, 1860-1954*

※

146 Man is the sickness, history the symptom.

※

147 All virtues are drawn from the well of courage.

> Courage is rightly esteemed the first of human qualities because it is the quality which guarantees all others.
> *Winston Churchill, 1874-1965*
>
> Courage is the ladder on which all the other virtues mount.
> *Clare Boothe Luce, 1903-1987*

148 Marriage is proof that people *can* learn to live with their mistakes.

☙

149 Diplomacy was invented by messengers.

☙

150 Keep smiling. You might get away with it.
> ... and one smile and smile and smile. And be a villain.
> *William Shakespeare, 1564-1616*

151 Laughter is the celebration of life, the language of transcendence, the salvation of the soul. Laugh often, live long.

> Laughter is the closest thing to the grace of God.
> *Karl Barth, 1886-1968*
>
> You don't stop laughing because you grow old;
> you grow old because you stop laughing.
> *Michael Pritchard, 1950—*

※

152 Sticks and stones can break my bones, but names are grounds for libel.

※

153 Creatures of habit need no cages.

> The chains of habit are too weak to be felt
> until they are too strong to be broken.
> *Samuel Johnson, 1709-1784*

154 When has righteous indignation *ever* had anything to do with being right?

> Moral indignation . . . permits envy or hate
> to be acted out under the guise of virtue.
> *Erich Fromm, 1900-1980*

※

155 As doctors and politicians know, people will swallow anything.

※

156 One of the most basic facts of life is that there is nothing basic about it.

157 Philosophy happens *after* dinner.
> Principles have no real force except when one is well fed.
> *Mark Twain, 1835-1910*
>
> Food comes first, then morals.
> *Bertolt Brecht, 1898-1956*

158 Politicians with the desire, means and brains to get elected should never be allowed in office.
> Whenever a man has cast a longing eye on office, a rottenness begins in his conduct.
> *Thomas Jefferson, 1743-1826*
>
> Anybody that wants the presidency so much that he'll spend two years organizing and campaigning for it is not to be trusted with the office.
> *David Broder, 1929-2011*

159 Anonymity and immunity have *always* been responsible for more truth than honesty and conscience.

160 If God can't make *His* children obey, what's a parent to do?

> I sometimes think that God, in creating man, somewhat overestimated His ability.
> *Oscar Wilde, 1854-1900*

※

161 Churchill coined the words, "Never have so many owed so much to so few." America made them an economic tradition.

※

162 Much of the world's most imaginative fiction has been written by historians.

> Very few things happen at the right time, and the rest do not happen at all; the conscientious historian will correct these defects.
> *Herodotus, 485-425 BC*
>
> The first qualification for a historian is to have no ability to invent.
> *Stendhal, 1783-1842*

163 Experts agree on the advisability of periodic truces in the war of the sexes—especially during the sex.

164 Democracy, like a majority, implies quantity over quality.

> When great changes occur in history, when great principles are involved, as a rule the majority are wrong.
> *Eugene V. Debs, 1855-1926*

165 Are people who speak in inspirational quotes simply trying to convince themselves?

166 Just because you *can* do it, doesn't mean you *should* do it.

> Science, which can do so much, cannot decide what it ought to do.
> *Joseph Wood Krutch, 1893-1970*
>
> What you might call technical arrogance . . . overcomes people when they see what they can do with their minds.
> *Freeman J. Dyson, 1923—*

※

167 Stupidity is incestuous. It breeds itself.

※

168 Laws are those annoying inconveniences you wish people who need them would be considerate enough to observe.

> Nothing so needs reforming as other people's habits.
> *Mark Twain, 1835-1910*
>
> The essence of immorality is the tendency to make an exception of myself.
> *Jane Addams, 1860-1935*

169 Man is the only animal that congratulates himself.

☙

170 The more superficial the man, the more indispensable the superfluous.

> Give us the luxuries of life and we will dispense with its necessities.
> *John Lothrop Motley, 1814-1877*
>
> The more outwardness, the less inwardness.
> *Soren Kierkegaard, 1813-1855*

☙

171 When politicians talk about the "greater good," they mean good for everybody but you.

172 How many Christians would want the God of the Bible for a father?

※

173 If variety is the spice of life, wouldn't that make monotony the main course?

> The joy of life is variety.
> *Samuel Johnson, 1709-1784*

※

174 More often than not, a broken heart is simply a bruised ego with no better options in sight.

175 As ends predispose means, so means predestine ends.

※

176 The vulgarity of the affluent lies in their manner, not their manners.

> I don't... want a lawyer to tell me what I cannot do.
> I hire him to tell me how to do what I want to do.
> *J. P. Morgan, 1837-1913*
>
> If you want to know what God thinks of
> money, just look at the people he gave it to.
> *Dorothy Parker, 1893-1967*

※

177 People smart enough to take advice usually don't need it.

> A word to the wise is sufficient.
> *Latin proverb*
>
> Wise men don't need advice. Fools won't take it.
> *Benjamin Franklin, 1706-1790*

178 Hate buries no hatchets—except for later use as concealed weapons.

☙

179 Problem Solving 101: Wait until the problem doesn't matter.

☙

180 The people who need kindness most usually deserve it least.

> Kindness consists in loving people more than they deserve.
> *Joseph Joubert, 1754-1824*
>
> If someone is too tired to give you a smile, leave one of your own, because no one needs a smile as much as those who have none to give.
> *Samson Raphael Hirsch, 1808-1888*

181 If everybody hates you, you're either doing something very wrong or very right.

☙

182 History is the record of fools getting in the way.

> History is indeed little more than the register of the crimes, follies, and misfortunes of mankind.
> *Edward Gibbon, 1737-1794*

☙

183 Why do politicians seem to expect diplomatic immunity in their own countries?

184 "The Lord giveth and the Lord taketh away."
Does that make the Lord an Indian giver?

> Fortune is fickle and soon asks back what he has given.
> *Latin proverb*

☙

185 The possibility of gender coexistence begins from the mutual understanding of the impossibility of mutual understanding.

☙

186 As humans so graphically demonstrate, survival of the fittest isn't always a force for the greater good.

187 Do those who lament loneliness at the top imagine good times for all on the bottom?

> Nothing is so hard for those who abound in
> riches as to conceive how others can be in want.
> *Jonathan Swift, 1667-1745*

❧

188 Who hasn't dreamed of filing a restraining order on reality?

❧

189 There is no stench so foul as the sweet smell of success on others.

> Whenever a friend succeeds, a little something in me dies.
> *Gore Vidal, 1925-2012*
>
> Men enjoy the inferiority of their best friends.
> *Philip Chesterfield, 1694-1773*

190 It's never too late to admit you're wrong, and always too early to insist you're right.

༼

191 Failure means at least you tried.

> A mistake means someone stopped
> talking long enough to do something.
> *Anonymous*
>
> It takes as much courage to have tried and
> failed as it does to have tried and succeeded.
> *Anne Morrow Lindbergh, 1906-2001*

༼

192 Necessity is the mother of invention, piracy and plagiarism the siblings.

193 Seldom do people talk more than when they have nothing to say.

> The less men think, the more they talk.
> *Montesquieu, 1689-1755*
> The thoughtless are rarely wordless.
> *Howard E. Newton*

※

194 The affectation of talent is often more profitable than its cultivation.

※

195 Nothing takes the fun out of a great idea like putting it into practice.

> It is a long road from conception to completion.
> *Molière, 1622-1673*

196 The most beautiful art is life well lived.

※

197 The general consensus in today's political circles seems to be that cluelessness is mitigated, if not rectified, by consistency.

> In politics stupidity is not a handicap.
> *Napoleon Bonaparte, 1769-1821*

※

198 Faith is hope that got religion.

> Our hope of immortality does not come from any religion, but nearly all religions come from that hope.
> *Robert G. Ingersoll, 1833-1899*

> Faith: not wanting to know what is true.
> *Friedrich Nietzsche, 1844-1900*

199 Relationships 101: "If you won't take me as I am, what about taking me as I *might* have been?"

※

200 Innocence is not a question of experience, but motive. A virgin saving herself to marry well is just prostitution in reverse.

> The truly innocent are those who not only are
> guiltless themselves, but who think others are.
> *Josh Billings, 1818-1885*

※

201 Money is like shit. Its primary uses are making things grow and getting thrown in people's faces.

> Money is like manure, of very little use except to be spread.
> *Francis Bacon, 1561-1626*
>
> Money is like manure. If you spread it around, it does a lot of good,
> but if you pile it up in one place, it stinks like hell.
> *Clinton W. Murchison, 1923-1987*

202 Children live what adults are reduced to acting out.

☙

203 Little fuels the fires of patriotism like the coals of prejudice.

> **Patriotism is the last refuge of a scoundrel.**
> *Samuel Johnson, 1709-1784*

☙

204 Naked truths, like naked emperors, lay bare what few wish to face.

205 Is it crueler to hurt people with lies or with the truth?

> A truth that's told with bad intent beats all the lies you can invent.
> *William Blake, 1757-1827*
>
> The man who is brutally honest enjoys the brutality quite as much as the honesty. Possibly more.
> *Richard J. Needham, 1912-1996*

※

206 To get people to do what *you* want them to do, tell them what *they* want to hear.

※

207 Life is too short to play fair.

208 How is it that, these days, everybody thinks they're entitled to the happiness without the pursuit?

> The U.S. Constitution doesn't guarantee happiness, only the pursuit of it. You have to catch up with it yourself.
> *Benjamin Franklin, 1706-1790*
>
> Don't go around saying the world owes you a living. The world owes you nothing. It was here first.
> *Mark Twain, 1835-1910*

☙

209 Relax. If God were dead, lawyers would be contesting the Estate.

☙

210 Childhood is that magic time of seeing what's not there and not seeing what is—that ensures children grow old without growing up.

211 The mind is mightier than the fact.

> The eyes are not responsible when the mind does the seeing.
> *Publilius Syrus, 46-29 BC*
> We do not see things the way they are. We see things the way we are.
> *Anonymous*

※

212 Property is the father of fear, the grandfather of government, and the ancestor of tyranny.

※

213 Politics 101: It's not fighting dirty if you win.

214  To sin is human. To escape undetected, divine.

※

215  Hate is little more than fear turned inside out.
> All cruelty springs from weakness.
> *Seneca, 4 BC-65 AD*
> Hatred is the coward's revenge for being intimidated.
> *George Bernard Shaw, 1856-1950*

※

216  Whoever said, "For every action, there's an equal and opposite reaction," never dated.

217 To the rich, life is a pissing contest using their tape measure.

※

218 Children should be available to the general public only with a doctor's prescription.

> Parentage is a very important profession; but no test of fitness for it is ever imposed in the interest of children.
> *George Bernard Shaw, 1856-1950*
>
> Parenthood remains the greatest single preserve of the amateur.
> *Alvin Toffler, 1928—*

※

219 Wisdom starts from knowing what matters.

> The wisdom of life consists in the elimination of nonessentials.
> *Lin Yutang, 1895-1976*
>
> It is not so important to be serious as it is to be serious about the important things.
> *Robert Maynard Hutchins, 1899-1977*

220 Mid-life crises are simply the early symptoms of late-life disasters.

℘

221 The first step to happiness is to stop believing you deserve it.

℘

222 The secret to appreciating pleasure is savoring in small bites, not devouring as if storing up fat for winter.

> Good things, when short, are twice as good.
> *Baltasar Gracián, 1601-1658*
>
> To make pleasures pleasant, shorten them.
> *Charles Buxton, 1823-1871*

223 If you can't beat 'em, sue 'em.

224 The best time to stay away from most people is when they're being themselves.

> "Be yourself" is about the worst advice you can give to some people.
> *Thomas Masson, 1866-1934*

225 There is nothing so dangerous as believers.

226 The secret of life is taking it as seriously as it takes you.

> Life is too important to be taken seriously.
> *Oscar Wilde, 1854-1900*
> No shred of evidence occurs in favor of the idea that life is serious.
> *Brendan Gill, 1914-1997*

༄

227 With the world in hopeless chaos, what's left for youth to rebel against?

༄

228 Good requires practice. Evil never loses its touch.

229 Beauty is as beauty does, and it's not always pretty.

> It is amazing how complete is the delusion that beauty is goodness.
> *Leo Tolstoy, 1828-1910*

230 No man is so creative as when making excuses.

231 People with a nose for conspiracy can sniff out anything but what's under it.

232 Pride boasts loudest of modesty.

> Pride, perceiving humility honorable, often borrows her cloak.
> *Thomas Fuller, 1608-1661*
>
> Modesty is my best quality.
> *Jack Benny, 1894-1974*

※

233 Life is the soap opera you can't turn off.

※

234 Is there an expiration date on the Second Coming?

235 There's more to success than just succeeding.

> Success has ruined many a man.
> *Benjamin Franklin, 1706-1790*
>
> The toughest thing about success is that you've got to keep on being a success.
> *Irving Berlin, 1888-1989*

❧

236 Has there ever been a connection between wealth and honor, except when the former buys the latter?

❧

237 Youth rails against what delays gratification, old age against what no longer matters.

238 Stupidity demands absolutes.

> Only a weak mind seeks ultimate answers.
> *Agnes Thornton, 1878-1939*

※

239 You're never happy caring what unhappy people think.

> Keep away from people who try to belittle your ambitions. Small people always do that.
> *Mark Twain, 1835-1910*

> To be happy, we must not be too concerned with others.
> *Albert Camus, 1913-1960*

※

240 Hope is wanting something you can't have—usually in inverse proportion to your chances of getting it.

> Hope: A pathological belief in the occurrence of the impossible.
> *H. L. Mencken, 1880-1956*

241 How long must you be subjected to daily doses of reality before you develop an immunity?

☙

242 A good start is making new mistakes.

> Every wrong attempt discarded is another step forward.
> *Thomas Edison, 1847-1931*
>
> If you're not failing every now and again,
> it's a sign you're not doing anything very innovative.
> *Woody Allen, 1935—*

☙

243 Acquired tastes are usually the prerogative of the acquisitive.

244   The atrocities of the Seven Deadly Sins pale by comparison to the barbarities of religion.

> More crimes have been committed in the name of Christ than in the name of the Devil.
> *Anonymous*

☙

245   Children are living proof that for every "no," there's a "why not?"

☙

246   Why is modern economy, that intricate balance of supply and demand, so seldom complicated by need?

247  The more cleverly we conceal our faults, the more righteously we revile them in others.

> If we had no faults, we would not take so much pleasure in noticing them in others.
> *François Duc de La Rochefoucauld, 1613-1680*
>
> Parents forgive their children least readily for the faults they themselves instilled in them.
> *Marie von Ebner-Eschenbach, 1830-1916*

※

248  Affluence answers to neither shame, honor nor law. Accountability is a poor man's curse.

> What do I care about the law? Ain't I got the power?
> *Cornelius Vanderbilt, 1794-1877*
>
> The public be damned.
> *William Henry Vanderbilt, 1821-1885*

※

249  Prejudice is a far crueler jailer than bars or chains.

250 To appreciate twists, you must be twisted.

☙

251 I'll wake up and smell the coffee when there's breakfast to go with it.

☙

252 Money doesn't just talk. It gets its @#$%&*! point across!

> Laws go where the dollars please.
> *Portuguese proverb*
> Money, like a queen, gives rank and beauty.
> *Latin proverb*

253 What conscience dictates, ego negotiates.

❧

254 Does history repeat itself when God can't come up with any new crises, scandals or disasters?

❧

255 Too many people find causes to die for because they can't find reasons to live for.

> It is easier to die for a cause than to live for it.
> *Hermann Hesse, 1877-1962*
>
> The mark of the immature man is that he wants to die nobly for a cause, while the mark of the mature man is that he wants to live humbly for one.
> *Wilhelm Stekel, 1868-1940*

256 If necessity is the mother of invention, is unnecessary invention the mother of advertising?

※

257 The secret of not failing lies in not attempting. Nothing ventured, nothing blown.

> It is only those who never do anything who never make mistakes.
> *Abraham Favre, 1685-1762*
>
> What isn't tried won't work.
> *Claude McDonald, 1852-1915*

※

258 Choose your challenges carefully. Not every wilderness comes with a promised land.

259 Far too often, little is more inhuman than human nature.

> **Man, I can assure you, is a nasty creature.**
> *Molière, 1622-1673*

෴

260 Acts of idiocy invariably bear the seeds of further idiocy.

෴

261 Life is perhaps the best example of the means failing to justify the end.

262 Is there no alternative but to leave politics to the politicians?

> Politics is too serious a matter to be left to the politicians.
> *Charles de Gaulle, 1890-1970*
>
> Government is too big and too important to be left to the politicians.
> *Chester Bowles, 1901-1986*

❧

263 The best things in life aren't free. You just pay in different currencies.

> The most important things in life aren't things.
> *Anonymous*

❧

264 Who programs kids to know what parents are least prepared for?

265 Historians write what they can't make.

> History is simply a piece of paper covered with print;
> the main thing is still to make history, not to write it.
> *Otto von Bismarck, 1815-1898*

℘

266 If the divorce rate teaches us anything, it's that practice does *not* make perfect.

℘

267 Is it happiness if you get it by making others unhappy?

> The pleasures of the rich are bought with the tears of the poor.
> *Thomas Fuller, 1608-1661*
> The white man's happiness cannot be purchased by the black man's misery.
> *Frederick Douglas, 1818-1895*

268 Hope springs eternal, which is why rational thinking doesn't.

> Hope muddies seeing.
> *Bert Bellinger, 1925—*

☙

269 People unable to overcome their own insecurities often make careers capitalizing on the insecurities of others.

> He who despises his own life is soon master of another's.
> *English proverb*

☙

270 Man has accomplished so much—that should never have been accomplished.

271 Sex is medicine's lone syndrome where the physical symptoms are the only known cure.

❧

272 Life 101: "By the time I'm ready to face the day, it's bedtime."

❧

273 It's impossible to reason with believers, small children and empty stomachs.

> A hungry stomach has no ears.
> *Jean de la Fontaine, 1621-1695*
>
> That which enters the mind through reason can be corrected. That which is admitted through faith, hardly ever.
> *Santiago Ramón y Cajal, 1852-1934*

274 What if life is just God's excuse to make shit happen?

≈

275 There is no wisdom like the wisdom of kindness and no kindness like the kindness of wisdom.

≈

276 The problem isn't that people don't *care* what *you* think, it's that they don't *know* what *they* think.

277 The truth might set you free, but it'll *never* make you rich.

> Honesty for the most part is less profitable than dishonesty.
> *Plato, 424-348 BC*
>
> The surest way to remain poor is to be an honest man.
> *Napoleon Bonaparte, 1769-1821*

※

278 Sometimes, the best solution is simply not compounding the problem.

> There is nothing so useless as doing efficiently that which should not be done at all.
> *Peter F. Drucker, 1909-2005*

※

279 If politicians really wanted to make a difference, they'd get out of politics.

280 The English language is an arsenal of weaponry to defeat opponents. Argument is war, discussion armed negotiation and communication strategic alliance.

> Language is the armory of the human mind; and at once contains the trophies of its past, and the weapons of its future conquests.
> *Samuel Taylor Coleridge, 1772-1834*
>
> To convince is to conquer without conception.
> *Benjamin Walter, 1892-1940*

※

281 In moving forward, the comforts of moderation must occasionally yield to the fury of excess.

> Even moderation ought not to be practiced to excess.
> *Anonymous*

※

282 Cultivate humility; it softens the blows when the world starts cultivating it for you.

> Life is a long lesson in humility.
> *James M. Barrie, 1860-1937*

283 A love affair with yourself is the best assurance of fidelity.

> He that falls in love with himself will have no rivals.
> *Benjamin Franklin, 1706-1790*
>
> Some of the greatest love affairs I've known involved one actor, unassisted.
> *Wilson Mizener, 1876-1933*

※

284 Life can be music if you play it by ear.

※

285 Once the meek inherit the earth, any bets on how long they remain meek?

> It's going to be fun to watch and see how long the meek can keep the earth after they inherit it.
> *Frank Hubbard, 1868-1930*

286 Understand yourself, and you understand others. Understand others, and you realize it wasn't worth the effort.

> The more one gets to know of men, the more one values dogs.
> *Alphonse Toussenel, 1803-1885*

❧

287 Relationships 101: Before you say anything, don't.

❧

288 Every individual is the exception *and* the rule.

> Always remember that you are absolutely unique. Just like everyone else.
> *Margaret Mead, 1901-1978*
>
> People have one thing in common: they are all different.
> *Robert Zend, 1929-1985*

289 What is man if not a bubbling cauldron of personalities unknown and undreamed of?

> We are ignorant of our own self and the depths within us.
> *Johannes Tauler, 1300-1361*
> Man can hardly even recognize the devils of his own creation.
> *Albert Schweitzer, 1875-1965*

290 The quickest way to many hearts is through an estate.

> The quickest way to a man's heart is through his chest.
> *Roseann Barr, 1952 —*

291 Talking a good game frequently obviates the necessity of playing it.

> The world steps aside for a man who acts like he knows where he's going.
> *D. S. Jordan, 1851-1931*
> You'd be surprised how often nerve succeeds.
> *Anonymous*

292  If idle hands are the Devil's playground,
misguided minds are His workshop.

> The Devil's name is dullness.
> *Robert E. Lee, 1807-1870*

❦

293  How did man end up the planet's only
overpopulated *and* endangered species?

❦

294  From the friction of argument come the sparks of
progress—marriage being the notable exception.

> Without contraries is no progression.
> *William Blake, 1757-1827*
> Ideas are kindled through friction.
> *Karol Bunsch, 1898-1987*

295 Just imagine if God decided to answer everyone's prayers at once!

※

296 Is too much of something better than almost enough of everything?

※

297 Justice is often unjust, but freedom is *never* free.

298 Man's greatest insult to God is boredom.

> Is not life a hundred times too short for us to bore ourselves?
> *Friedrich Nietzsche, 1844-1900*

※

299 Procrastination is most regrettable in cases of kindness, because the time for kindness is always right.

> You cannot do a kindness too soon, for you never know how soon it will be too late.
> *Ralph Waldo Emerson, 1803-1882*
>
> The time is always right to do what is right.
> *Martin Luther King, Jr., 1929-1968*

※

300 "Talent" is often just the ability to show off better than everyone else.

301 Hell is full of creative thinkers. Who improvises better than sinners?

❧

302 Knowledge is learned, wisdom earned.
> Knowledge can be communicated, but not wisdom.
> *Hermann Hesse, 1877-1962*

❧

303 A silver tongue speaks not from the heart.
> When there is a gap between one's real and one's declared aims, one turns as if it were instinctively to long words and exhausted idioms, like a cuttlefish squirting out ink.
> *William A. Orton, 1889-1952*

304 There is no "level playing field" in the game of love.

☙

305 Most people spend their lives looking for diversions from life.
> Most of one's life ... is one prolonged effort to prevent oneself thinking.
> *Aldous Huxley, 1894-1963*
>
> We live in what is, but we find 1,000 ways not to face it.
> *Thornton Wilder, 1897-1975*

☙

306 Lending desires return, borrowing poor memory.
> The creditor hath a better memory than the debtor.
> *James Howell, 1594-1666*

307 Love's milestones are the best calendar.

۶

308 We see ourselves in what we want and want ourselves in what we see.

۶

309 You can be a friend to others only by doing the same to yourself.

> He who is his own friend is a friend to all men.
> *Seneca, 4 BC-65 AD*
> The only way to have a friend is to be one.
> *Ralph Waldo Emerson, 1803-1882*

310  If all the great wisdom has, in fact, been said, it proves nobody was listening.

☙

311  No greater acumen *or* discipline is required than knowing when to say, "When!" to a good thing.

> To many, total abstinence is easier than perfect moderation.
> *Saint Augustine, 354-430*
> It is easier to suppress the first desire than to satisfy all that follow it.
> *Benjamin Franklin, 1706-1790*

☙

312  There are no speed limits on the road to ruin.

313 If someone has nothing to lose, do you trust him more or less?

> **Beware the person with nothing to lose.**
> *Italian proverb*

❧

314 If man had the same track record in technology as in marriage, we'd still be stuck in the Stone Age.

❧

315 Hollywood prayer: "Dear God, what have you done for me lately?"

316 The richer the man, the dirtier the hands.
> A rich man is either a scoundrel or the heir of a scoundrel.
> *Spanish proverb*
>
> Behind every great fortune lies a great crime.
> *Honoré de Balzac, 1799-1850*

☙

317 If you look at love as a game, you're the loser.

☙

318 Differences are unavoidable. Marriage makes them irreconcilable.

319 We've all been hurt. The question is, do we hurt others more or less as a result?

> It's usually the most wounded among us who inflict pain on others.
> *Patti Davis, 1952—*

※

320 The more people thank you for what they get from you today, the more they'll want from you tomorrow.

> The gratitude of most men is but a secret desire of receiving greater benefits.
> *François Duc de La Rochefoucauld, 1613-1680*

※

321 The religious pray. It's the devout who refuse to take "no" for an answer.

> Father expected a good deal from God. He didn't actually accuse God of inefficiency, but when he prayed his tone was loud and angry, like that of a dissatisfied guest in a carelessly managed hotel.
> *Clarence Day, 1874-1935*

322 $K$nowing your options *can* be the cruelest punishment.

> Children's talent to endure stems from their ignorance of alternatives.
> *Maya Angelou, 1928-2014*

☙

323 $N$ature is just God showing off.

☙

324 $H$ow quickly men rush to sell their souls upon hearing those magic words, "something for nothing."

> One of the best ways to measure people is to watch the way they behave when something free is offered.
> *Ann Landers, 1918-2002*

325 Getting even never really makes it that way.

> No revenge is more honorable than the one not taken.
> *Spanish proverb*
>
> Revenge has no more quenching effect
> on emotions than salt water has on thirst.
> *Walter Weckler*

326 All truth is inconvenient.

> If you speak the truth have a foot in the stirrup.
> *Turkish proverb*
>
> A remark generally hurts in proportion to its truth.
> *Will Rogers, 1879-1935*

327 If your cup runneth over, just get a bigger cup!

328 The strongest marriage bonds are often compatible neuroses.

※

329 Life is the art of taking chances.

> Risk-taking is inherently failure-prone.
> Otherwise it would be called sure-thing-taking.
> *Tim McMahon*
>
> "Why not" is a slogan for an interesting life.
> *Mason Cooley, 1927-2002*

※

330 Most people are never old enough to know better.

331 Politicians have succeeded where anarchists failed—in plunging the world into anarchy.

❦

332 Wisdom includes knowing when to play the fool.

> It is a profitable thing, if one is wise, to seem foolish.
> *Aeschylus, 5th century BC*
> The height of cleverness is to be able to conceal it.
> *François Duc de La Rochefoucauld, 1613-1680*

❦

333 In matters of the gods, myth is the page, magic the pen.

334  Innocence and guilt are two sides of the same coin, depending on which judge gets the coin.

※

335  Life is an ongoing exercise in the lowering of expectations.

※

336  Those who live for the hunt rarely savor the kill.

> An object in possession seldom retains the same charm it had in pursuit.
> *Pliny the Younger, 1st century BC*
>
> We think about sex obsessively except during the act, when our minds tend to wander.
> *Howard Nemerov, 1920-1991*

337 After repeated, demoralizing setbacks, only courageous heroes and hopeless losers come back for more.

༄

338 No one *chooses* to be governed.

༄

339 Man is the animal that evolves, but doesn't learn.

340 The less you remember, the more fun you must've had.

> One reason I don't drink is that I want to know when I'm having a good time.
> *Anonymous*

☙

341 People with nothing more than the sense to shut up have quite a bit.

> Nothing is more like a wise man than a fool who holds his tongue.
> *Saint Francis de Sales, 1567-1622*
>
> Never miss a good chance to shut up.
> *Will Rogers, 1879-1935*

☙

342 Do more milestones of achievement come from the search for meaning or the flight from boredom?

> The life of the creative man is led, directed and controlled by boredom. Avoiding boredom is one of our most important purposes.
> *Saul Steinberg, 1914-1999*

343 The more freedoms people enjoy, the more they imagine they're missing out on.

⁂

344 Is what psychiatry calls "neurosis" just man's socially unacceptable attempts to solve society's unsolvable problems?

⁂

345 If people tried to change themselves and not society, there'd be no need for a society to change.

> Everybody thinks of changing humanity and
> nobody thinks of changing himself.
> *Leo Tolstoy, 1828-1910*

346  Wise men come and go, but fools are forever.

☙

347  One sure way to go down in history is to take lots of people with you.

☙

348  Courage doesn't always come with pomp and bravado. Sometimes it's just getting up in the morning.

> Any idiot can face a crisis;
> it's this day-to-day living that wears you out.
> *Anton Chekhof, 1860-1904*

349 Talking dirty says more in body language.

⁂

350 Ever wish you could hire a bodyguard to protect you from yourself?

⁂

351 Few things are more dangerous than a man stripped of his illusions.

> Nothing is more sad than the death of an illusion.
> *Arthur Koestler, 1905-1983*
>
> Nobody knows what's in him until he tries to pull it out. If there's nothing, or very little, the shock can kill a man.
> *Ernest Hemingway, 1899-1961*

352 Beware the man who must convince the world.

※

353 As the kindest word often goes unspoken, so the most heartfelt gift often goes ungiven.
> Nothing is often a good thing to do and always a clever thing to say.
> *Will Durant, 1885-1981*

※

354 If you don't know why you're doing something, do you really know *what* you're doing?

355 Man fights for everything except what's worth fighting for.

※

356 How many times have you given your heart, only to end up feeling like an organ donor?

> Every time I gave my word, I never saw it again.
> *Roberto Gervaso, 1937 —*

※

357 Nothing becomes the Devil's work faster than the word of God in the hands of morons.

358 Self-praise is always the most sincere.

> The advantage of doing one's praising for oneself is that
> one can lay it on thick and exactly in the right places.
> *Samuel Butler, 1835-1902*
>
> When a man gets talking about himself, he seldom fails
> to be eloquent and often reaches the sublime.
> *Josh Billings, 1818-1885*

359 When the truth hurts too much to bear, the most effective analgesic is often blind, unquestioning love.

360 Does "progress" exist simply because humanity can't leave well enough alone?

> What we call "progress" is the exchange of one nuisance for another nuisance.
> *Havelock Ellis, 1859-1939*

361 People who'll do anything to grab the spotlight are precisely the ones to keep out of it.

※

362 Money costs.

> A great fortune is a great slavery.
> *Seneca, 4 BC-65 AD*
>
> We can have democracy in this country or we can have great wealth concentrated in the hands of the few, but we can't have both.
> *Louis D. Brandeis, 1856-1941*

※

363 Few words are dearer to those who never learn than "next time."

364 Envy is the most cowardly form of surrender.

> The dullard's envy of brilliant men is always assuaged
> by the suspicion that they will come to a bad end.
> *John Beecher, 1904-1980*

※

365 The ability to see wonder in the commonplace rests on the understanding that nothing is common.

> To be alive, to be able to see, to walk, to have houses,
> music, paintings—it's all a miracle. I have adopted the
> technique of living life from miracle to miracle.
> *Artur Rubinstein, 1887-1982*

> Normal day, let me be aware of the treasure you are.
> *Mary Jean Irion*

※

366 All thinking is wishful, all conquest vanity.

367 Man defines himself by what he wants and how far he's willing to go to get it.

※

368 Guilt is temptations succumbed to, regret temptations resisted.

※

369 A man is always eager to learn from his last misstep until he extricates his foot from the hole.

> The wolf was sick, he vowed a monk to be,
> but when he got well, a wolf once more was he.
> *Walter Bower, 1385-1449*

370 Ever felt like your heart is an open book no one wants to read between the lines?

※

371 Man is the animal that makes life harder by making it easier.

> When Consumer Reports begins to describe the potential for dire calamity that lies behind most everyday activities, my hands tremble, my vision blurs, and I have to go lie quietly for a while.
> *Colin McEnroe, 1954—*
>
> Progress is man's ability to complicate simplicity.
> *Thor Heyerdahl, 1914-2002*

※

372 Is narcissism its own reward?

373 Taste is acquired only by tasting.

> The knowledge of the world is only to be
> acquired in the world, and not in a closet.
> *Philip Chesterfield, 1694-1773*
>
> The only way to discover the limits of the possible
> is to venture a little way past them into the impossible.
> *Arthur C. Clarke, 1917-2008*

☙

374 Thank goodness women lack the physical strength of predatory animals.

> A woman is the only thing I am afraid of that I know will not hurt me.
> *Abraham Lincoln, 1809-1865*
>
> Women keep a special corner of their hearts for sins they have never committed.
> *Cornelia Otis Skinner, 1899-1979*

☙

375 Passion cannot be taught. Does a fire learn to burn?

376 Many of the fiercest combatants in the war of the sexes swear they're on the same side.

> Nobody will ever win the battle of the sexes.
> There's too much fraternizing with the enemy.
> *Henry Kissinger, 1923 —*
>
> It is hard to fight an enemy who has outposts in your head.
> *Sally Kempton*

※

377 Breeding, education and technology simply furnish fools and villains more pernicious options.

> If the human race wants to go to hell in a basket,
> technology can help it get there by jet.
> *Charles Mengel Allen, 1916-2000*
>
> A man who has never gone to school may steal from a freight car;
> but if he has a university education, he may steal the whole railroad.
> *Theodore Roosevelt, 1858-1919*

※

378 There is no good or bad in stupid.

379 In this world of conflicting wisdom, how do you know when to look before you leap and when you'll be lost if you hesitate?

☙

380 Running away from your problems won't solve them, but it sure beats *facing* them.

> No problem is too big to run away from.
> *Charles M. Schulz, 1922-2000*

☙

381 The wisest of the wise remain hidden in plain sight, because it takes one to know one.

> The world knows nothing of its greatest men.
> *Henry Taylor, 1800-1886*
> It requires wisdom to understand wisdom.
> *Walter Lippman, 1889-1974*

382 Logic, rationality and objectivity only go so far. From there, it's pride, greed and lust for power.

☙

383 The more you look in mirrors, the less likely you like what you see.

☙

384 Dirty minds think more.

> An indecent mind is a perpetual feast.
> *Old saying*
> Below the navel there is neither religion nor truth.
> *Italian Proverb*

385 Relationships 101: "I may be easy, but I'm not cheap."

※

386 Cynicism is the curse of those who hate to be right.

> Cynicism is that blackguard defect of vision which compels us to see the world as it is, instead of as it should be.
> *Ambrose Bierce, 1842-1914*
>
> Cynicism is an unpleasant way of saying the truth.
> *Lillian Hellman, 1905-1984*

※

387 Optimism is like the air in a tire with a slow leak. Running out is just a question of miles.

> Optimists and pessimists differ only on the date of the end of the world.
> *Stanislaw Jerzy Lec, 1909-1966*

388 Absence might make the heart grow fonder, though not necessarily of the absentee.

> If you can't be with the one you love, love the one you're with.
> *Stephen Stills, 1945—*

₰

389 Many times, what passes for courage is just panic with eyes closed and fingers crossed.

> Endurance is frequently a form of indecision.
> *Elizabeth Bibesco, 1897-1945*
>
> Our strength is often composed of the weaknesses we're damned if we're going to show.
> *Mignon McLaughlin, 1913-1983*

₰

390 The approach of philosophy is to question everything, except the approach of philosophy.

391 Morality is making sure no one else is getting what you're not.

※

392 Hating the world is the punishment for the crime of hating yourself.

> **Hatred is self-punishment.**
> *Hosea Ballou, 1771-1852*
> **He who hates, hates himself.**
> *Southern African saying*

※

393 Is abstinence easier or harder once you know what you're missing?

394 Relationships 101: "Where were you when I needed you? And why are you always here when I don't?"

> Failing to be there when a man wants her is a woman's greatest sin, except to be there when he doesn't want her.
> *Helen Rowland, 1875-1950*
>
> The fickleness of the women I love is only equaled by the infernal consistency of the women who love me.
> *George Bernard Shaw, 1856-1950*

※

395 The easily bored are usually just as boring.

> When people are bored, it is primarily with their own selves.
> *Eric Hoffer, 1902-1983*
>
> A healthy male bore consumes each year one and a half times his own weight in other people's patience.
> *John Updike, 1932-2009*

※

396 If you can't get what you want by ordinary means, declare it a God-given right.

397 Bravado and ignorance are, theoretically, mutually exclusive bedfellows that, in practice, rule the world.

※

398 The mind can hold so much that means so little.

> A great deal of learning can be packed into an empty head.
> *Karl Kraus, 1874-1936*
>
> A man can believe a considerable amount of rubbish, and yet go about his daily work in a rational and cheerful manner.
> *Norman Douglas, 1868-1952*

※

399 In creativity lies a magical return to childhood, when *every* act was an act of creation.

> Every child is an artist. The problem is how to remain an artist once he grows up.
> *Pablo Picasso, 1881-1973*
>
> No matter how old you get, if you keep the desire to be creative, you're keeping the man-child alive.
> *John Cassavetes, 1929-1989*

400 The ultimate art is dying. It takes a lifetime.

> The art of living well and the art of dying well are one.
> *Epicurus, 341-270 BC*
>
> One should ever be booted and spurred and ready to depart.
> *Michel Eyquem de Montaigne, 1533-1592*

# Special Thanks

I'd like to give a heartfelt shout-out to the following friends and acquaintances for their assistance:

*Larry Zook* for above-and-beyond intro editing and all-round collaboration

*John Klingler, Charles Owens, Cole Russing* and *Walter Roberts* for manuscript assessment and advice

*Monique Stensrud*, without whom, on many levels, this edition would never happened

# Author Index

Addams, Jane   70
Aeschylus   125
Allen, Charles Mengel   140
Allen, Woody   46, 95
Angelou, Maya   122
Augustine, Saint   118

Bacon, Francis   81
Ballou, Hosea   145
Barrie, James M.   108
Barrymore, Ethyl   48
Barth, Karl   65
Baudelaire, Charles   26
Beecher, John   136
Bellinger, Bert   104
Bennett, Arnold   56
Benny, Jack   92
Berlin, Irving   93
Bibesco, Elizabeth   144
Bierce, Ambrose   143
Billings, Josh   12, 42, 81, 134
Blake, William   33, 83, 112

Bonaparte, Napoleon   80, 107
Boulding, Kenneth Ewart   20
Bourguiba, Habib   48
Bower, Walter   137
Bowles, Chester   102
Brandeis, Louis D.   135
Bradley, F. H.   63
Brecht, Bertolt   67
Brickman, Morrie   24
Broder, David   67
Bruyère, Jean de la   17
Bulwer-Lytton, Edward   54
Bunsch, Karol   112
Burns, Ron   61
Butler, Samuel   134
Buxton, Charles   88

Cajal, Santiago Ramón y   105
Camus, Albert   94
Carlyle, Thomas   52
Cassavetes, John   147
Chanel, Coco   47

Chaplin, Charles   28
de Chateaubriand,
   François-René   5
Chekhof, Anton   130
Chesterfield, Philip   77, 139
Chesterton, G. K.   60
Chopin, Dan   24
Churchill, Winston   63
Ciardi, John   2
Clarke, Arthur C.   139
Cocteau, Jean   1
Coleridge, Samuel Taylor   108
Colton, Charles Caleb   40, 41
Cooley, Mason   124
Cosby, Bill   16

Davis, Patti   121
Day, Clarence   121
de Balzac, Honoré   120
de Gaulle, Charles   57, 102
de Sales, Saint Francis   128
de la Fontaine, Jean   105
Debs, Eugene V.   69
Dickens, Charles   52

Douglas, Frederick   103
Douglas, Norman   147
Drucker, Peter F.   107
Dunker, Thomas   17
Durant, Will   132
Dyson, Freeman J.   70

Edison, Thomas   95
Eliot, George   37
Ellis, Havelock   134
Emerson, Ralph Waldo   41, 43, 53, 114, 117
Epicurus   148
Euripides   18, 35

Favre, Abraham   100
Franklin, Benjamin   73, 84, 93, 109, 118
Fromm, Erich   66
Frost, Robert   16
Froude, James Anthony   39
Fuller, R. Buckminster   7
Fuller, Thomas   23, 92, 103

Galbraith, John Kenneth  58
Gary, Romain  52
Gervaso, Roberto  133
Gibbon, Edward  75
Gill, Brendan  90
Goethe, Johann Wolfgang
    von  15, 31, 42
Gracián, Baltasar  88
Gregory, Dick  56

Hamilton, Robert B.  38
Havoc, June  30
Hellman, Lillian  143
Hemingway, Ernest  131
Herodotus  68
Hesse, Hermann  99, 115
Heyerdahl, Thor  48, 138
Hirsch, Samson Raphael  74
Hoffenstein, Samuel  62
Hoffer, Eric  33, 146
Howell, James  116
Hubbard, Frank  109
Hutchins, Robert Maynard  87
Huxley, Aldous  55, 116

Inge, William Ralph  63
Ingersoll, Robert G.  80
Irion, Mary Jean  136

Jefferson, Thomas  67
Johnson, Samuel  4, 15, 65,
    72, 82
Jordan, D. S.  111
Joubert, Joseph  74

Kempton, Sally  140
Kierkegaard, Soren  71
King, Martin Luther, Jr.  114
Kissinger, Henry  140
Koestler, Arthur  131
Kraus, Karl  13, 147
Kronenberger, Louis  34
Krutch, Joseph Wood  70
Kurz, Isolde  52

Lance, Thomas Bertram  1
Landers, Ann  122
Leach, Robin  36
Lec, Stanislaw Jerzy  143

Lee, Robert E. 112
Lin, Yutang 34, 87
Lincoln, Abraham 139
Lindbergh, Anne Morrow 78
Lippman, Walter 141
Luce, Clare Boothe 63

Marx, Groucho 36
Masson, Thomas 89
May, Rollo 25
McDonald, Claude 100
McEnroe, Colin 138
McLaughlin, Mignon 144
McMahon, Tim 124
Mead, Margaret 110
Mencken, H. L. 9, 94
Michelangelo 53
Miller, Milton H. 56
Mizener, Wilson 109
Molière 79, 101
Montaigne, Michel Eyquem de 49, 50, 53, 58, 148
Montesquieu 79
Morgan, J. P. 73

Motley, John Lothrop 71
Murchison, Clinton W. 81

Needham, Richard J. 83
Nehru, Jawaharlal 36
Nemerov, Howard 126
Newton, Howard E. 79
Nietzsche, Friedrich 59, 80, 114

Orwell, George 39
Orton, William A. 115
Ovid 49

Parker, Dorothy 73
Paronen, Samuli 61
Pascal, Blaise 38
Picasso, Pablo 147
Pierce, Franklin 21
Plato 107
Pliny the Younger 126
Powell, Anthony 29
Pritchard, Michael 65
Progoff, Ira 29
Publilius Syrus 85

Raleigh, Walter 35
Rand, Ayn 54
Renard, Jules 30
Rochefoucauld, François, Duc de La 43, 97, 121, 125
Rogers, Will 123, 128
Roosevelt, Theodore 140
Rowland, Helen 146
Rubinstein, Artur 136
Russell, Bertand 5

Sarraute, Nathalie 45
Schulz, Charles M. 141
Schweitzer, Albert 111
Seneca 86, 117, 135
Shakespeare, William 64
Shankly, Bill 39
Shaw, George Bernard 86, 87, 146
Sheed, Wilfrid 47
Skinner, Cornelia Otis 139
Smith, Sydney 22
Steinberg, Saul 128
Stekel, Wilhelm 99

Stendhal 68
Stevenson, Adlai 28
Stills, Stephen 144
Swift, Jonathan 77

Tauler, Johannes 111
Taylor, Henry 141
Taylor, Jeremy 46
Terence 30
Thoene, Bodie 22
Thornton, Agnes 94
Toffler, Alvin 87
Tolstoy, Leo 91, 129
Toussenel, Alphonse 110
Twain, Mark 9, 14, 31, 67, 70, 84, 94

Updike, John 146

Vanderbilt, Cornelius 97
Vanderbilt, William Henry 97
Vaughan, Harry 26
Vidal, Gore 77

von Bismarck, Otto  103
von Ebner-Eschenbach, Marie  97

Walter, Benjamin  108
Weckler, Walter  123
Whitehead, Alfred North  56
Wilde, Oscar  68, 90
Wilder, Thornton  116
Wilson, Edward O.  48

Zend, Robert  110

# The Author

*(Photo by Takaaki Iwabu)*

Gordon Hutchison spent thirty years in Japan on what started out as the first stop on a trip around the world. After three years at a Zen monastery, he went on to specialize in Japanese folk religions at Sophia Graduate School of International Studies, teach Hatha yoga in Japanese and log twenty-four years as a copywriter—four at the world's largest ad agency and the rest at the smallest, his own. He lives with his eighteen-year-old son Evan in Cary, North Carolina.